Hybrid Comp

Harnessing Next-Generation Performance and AI Power

Taylor Royce

DEDICATION

This book is devoted to the visionaries, educators, and inventors who never stop pushing the limits of knowledge and technology. This work is for everyone who questions the status quo, encourages curiosity, and dedicates their lives to creating a better future for everybody.

Additionally, it is dedicated to my family and loved ones, whose steadfast encouragement and support have been a continual source of strength for me during this journey. Every obstacle has been worthwhile because of your faith in me.

Finally, I dedicate this book to everyone who still believes in education, personal development, and the limitless potential of exploration. I hope these pages inspire you to discover, create, and leave your own impression on the world.

DISCLAIMER

This book contains information that should only be used for general informative purposes. Although every attempt has been taken to guarantee the content's accuracy and dependability, the author and publisher make no guarantees or representations about the information's suitability, accuracy, or completeness.

The opinions and viewpoints presented in this book are those of the author and may not represent the official stance or policy of any institution, business, or organization that the author is connected to.

This book's information is not meant to be used as expert counsel or advice. Before making decisions based on the information supplied, readers are urged to consult with relevant specialists or obtain expert advice.

Any losses, damages, or other outcomes resulting from the use or reliance on the material in this book are not the responsibility of the author or publisher.

Hybrid Computing

CONTENTS

ACKNOWLEDGMENTS

I want to sincerely thank everyone who has helped me along the way as I've been writing this book. Without the direction, inspiration, and steadfast assistance of many people, this endeavor would not have been feasible.

First and foremost, I want to express my gratitude to my family for their unending support and affection. Your confidence in me, even when I doubted myself, has always inspired me. I want to express my gratitude to my friends for being my sounding board and for constantly pushing me to think more creatively and boldly. You have given me perspective and motivation.

I am also incredibly appreciative of the experts, mentors, and colleagues that contributed their knowledge and experience to this work by sharing their ideas and expertise. Your input has enabled me to hone concepts and offer a more thorough analysis of the topic.

We would especially want to thank the readers and community members who are always looking to expand their knowledge and push the limits of creativity. Your insatiable curiosity and quest for advancement are what will shape education and technology in the future.

Last but not least, I want to thank the editorial and publishing staff for their tremendous efforts, whose meticulous attention to detail and dedication to quality made this book possible.

I want to express my gratitude to everyone who helped along the way, no matter how tiny, for your tremendous support. Your support and cooperation are evident in this book.

CHAPTER 1

AN OVERVIEW OF HYBRID COMPUTING

1.1 A Comprehensive Overview of Hybrid Computing

A significant development in computational science and technology is hybrid computing. Hybrid computing aims to minimize the drawbacks of various systems while maximizing their strengths by fusing several computing paradigms. Let's dissect this in more detail:

Hybrid Computing: Definition and Importance

Fundamentally, hybrid computing is an architectural strategy that combines several computing models into a single framework, such as general-purpose CPUs and GPUs, cloud and on-premise systems, or classical and quantum systems. These systems can work together seamlessly thanks to this integration, which guarantees that computational activities are assigned to the most effective platform according to their particular needs.

By providing scalability, flexibility, and performance optimization, hybrid computing is significant because it can manage increasingly complex computational difficulties across a range of industries, from artificial intelligence to healthcare.

A summary of the computing paradigms that are incorporated into hybrid systems

Conventional CPU-based computing is frequently combined with specialist hardware such as GPUs, TPUs (Tensor computing Units), and even quantum processors in hybrid systems. A closer look is as follows:

- **Cloud and On-Premise Systems:** Hybrid computing frequently provides scalability without sacrificing control over sensitive data by bridging the gap between local infrastructure and cloud-based resources.

- **Classical and Quantum Systems:** Hybrid computing allows for innovative solutions in both research and industry by utilizing classical systems for general-purpose activities and integrating quantum computing for jobs like molecular simulation or cryptography analysis.

CHAPTER 1

An Overview of Hybrid Computing

1.1 A Comprehensive Overview of Hybrid Computing

A significant development in computational science and technology is hybrid computing. Hybrid computing aims to minimize the drawbacks of various systems while maximizing their strengths by fusing several computing paradigms. Let's dissect this in more detail:

Hybrid Computing: Definition and Importance

Fundamentally, hybrid computing is an architectural strategy that combines several computing models into a single framework, such as general-purpose CPUs and GPUs, cloud and on-premise systems, or classical and quantum systems. These systems can work together seamlessly thanks to this integration, which guarantees that computational activities are assigned to the most effective platform according to their particular needs.

2

By providing scalability, flexibility, and performance optimization, hybrid computing is significant because it can manage increasingly complex computational difficulties across a range of industries, from artificial intelligence to healthcare.

A summary of the computing paradigms that are incorporated into hybrid systems

Conventional CPU-based computing is frequently combined with specialist hardware such as GPUs, TPUs (Tensor computing Units), and even quantum processors in hybrid systems. A closer look is as follows:

- **Cloud and On-Premise Systems:** Hybrid computing frequently provides scalability without sacrificing control over sensitive data by bridging the gap between local infrastructure and cloud-based resources.

- **Classical and Quantum Systems:** Hybrid computing allows for innovative solutions in both research and industry by utilizing classical systems for general-purpose activities and integrating quantum computing for jobs like molecular simulation or cryptography analysis.

- **Edge and Cloud Computing:** A harmonious balance is achieved by using cloud resources for more complex calculations and edge devices for local real-time data processing.

Value in Addressing Complicated Computational Issues

When specialized computation or huge parallelism are needed, hybrid computing performs exceptionally well. For instance, in artificial intelligence, hybrid systems effectively train and implement complex models by fusing cloud-based machine learning platforms with the raw processing power of GPUs. In a similar vein, hybrid systems in climate modeling employ a variety of computer resources to examine complex atmospheric data at scale.

1.2 Development of Paradigms in Computing

Knowing how computing paradigms have changed throughout time helps explain why hybrid computing has become essential in today's technological environment.

Historical Computing Technology Milestones

Over the years, computing has undergone an amazing

journey:

- The mainframe period of the 1950s and 1960s was characterized by centralized computing.
- The emergence of personal computers in the 1970s and 1980s democratized access to computing power.
- 1990s: Distributed computing and networked systems were introduced with the introduction of the internet.
- 2000s: Scalable, on-demand resource access was made possible by the rise of cloud computing.
- 2010s and Beyond: The computational paradigm started to change as a result of AI, machine learning, and quantum computing.

Move from Conventional to Advanced Models of Computing

Although mainframes and standalone systems, two examples of old computing architectures, provided fundamental capabilities, contemporary demands required a shift to more sophisticated frameworks. While GPUs transformed processing for applications like gaming, artificial intelligence, and data analytics, cloud computing brought elastic scalability.

The result of this shift is hybrid computing, which combines these developments to overcome the drawbacks of solo or compartmentalized models.

The function of hybrid computing in the advancement of modern technology

Hybrid computing fills the gaps between systems that used to function independently in today's networked society. It has enabled innovations in fields such as:

- **Healthcare:** By integrating cloud-powered data aggregation for medical diagnostics with local AI analysis on edge devices.
- **Finance:** Facilitating high-frequency trading systems that depend on real-time centralized risk analysis and low-latency edge processing.
- **Energy:** Cloud analytics and IoT sensors are integrated for effective energy management.

1.3 The Significance of Hybrid Computing in the Present

Hybrid computing is becoming more and more relevant because it can solve the urgent problems of contemporary computing while opening up previously unheard-of possibilities for innovation.

The need for high-performance computing is increasing.

The computing systems used in today's businesses must be able to process enormous volumes of data accurately and quickly.

- Large datasets and training cycles are necessary for AI and machine learning models, which make use of hybrid systems' parallel processing capabilities.
- The supercomputing power required for scientific study, such climate modeling and genomics, can only be supplied via hybrid architectures.

Single-Paradigm Computing Challenges

Conventional single-paradigm computing systems frequently encounter major limitations:

- **Scalability:** Cloud-only solutions may result in latency and cost inefficiencies, while on-premise systems have trouble handling elastic demand.
- **Specialization:** One paradigm could not have the specialized hardware or software required for

specific activities, such as using CPUs to execute AI algorithms rather than GPUs or TPUs.

- **Integration:** Data processing and transfer are inefficient when siloed systems are unable to work together.

using merging paradigms into coherent systems that allow tasks to be completed using the best available resources, hybrid computing tackles these issues.

Hybrid Approaches Open Up Opportunities

The hybrid model has revolutionary advantages, such as:

- **Cost Optimization:** While keeping on-premise systems for routine operations, organizations can use cloud resources for periods of high demand.
- **Enhanced Security and Compliance:** While less important tasks are transferred to the cloud, sensitive data might stay on local systems.
- **Agility and Flexibility:** Developers can move to cloud systems for in-depth batch processing and employ edge computing for real-time analytics.
- **Interdisciplinary Advancements:** Hybrid systems allow for advances in material science,

cryptography, and other fields by combining classical and quantum computing.

The way we tackle computational problems has drastically changed as a result of hybrid computing. It overcomes the constraints of conventional systems and creates opportunities for innovation across industries by combining several paradigms. Comprehending its fundamentals, development, and importance equips us to capitalize on its potential for a future that is more technologically sophisticated, efficient, and interconnected.

CHAPTER 2

ESSENTIAL HYBRID COMPUTING ELEMENTS

The integration of several components, each of which adds to the hybrid computing system's performance and versatility, is what makes it thrive. The fundamental components that allow hybrid systems to operate smoothly and effectively are examined in this chapter.

2.1 Calculation Methods

The core of hybrid computing is computational power, and utilizing the advantages of several processing units is essential to its success. Let's look at the main compute mechanisms and what they do:

The Functions of Central Processing Units (CPUs)

Known as the "brains" of a computer, CPUs are essential to hybrid systems. They are excellent at conducting general-purpose calculations and carrying out sequential activities.

- **Versatility:** CPUs are essential in hybrid configurations because they can handle a broad range of applications, including operating systems and user interfaces.

- **Efficiency:** Because modern CPUs have numerous cores, they can execute tasks concurrently, which is crucial when dividing workloads among hybrid environments.

- **Control:** CPUs frequently serve as orchestrators in hybrid systems, overseeing and assigning work to additional specialized processors like GPUs or ASICs.

Graphics Processing Units (GPUs) for Computation in Parallel

In hybrid computing systems, GPUs specialized processors made for parallel processing are essential for managing compute-intensive activities.

- **Parallelism:** GPUs are perfect for machine learning, scientific simulations, and rendering workloads because they can do thousands of processes at once.

- **Integration:** GPUs are used by hybrid systems,

frequently in combination with CPUs, to speed up particular tasks. For example, while CPUs oversee tasks, GPUs do data-intensive calculations for AI training models.

- **Emerging Technologies:** GPUs are being utilized more and more in decentralized hybrid systems, like blockchain networks, where they help with transaction validation and hash computations.

Neuromorphic chips and ASICs are examples of specialized processors

Specialized processors are essential for maximizing performance for specialized applications as hybrid computing develops:

- **Application-Specific Integrated Circuits (ASICs):** These chips are designed to perform certain functions, such high-speed data compression or cryptocurrency mining. They are useful in hybrid systems where specialization is necessary due to their efficiency.

- **Chips that are neuromorphic:** These processors are made for artificial intelligence activities, especially in edge computing settings where making decisions in real time is crucial. They are inspired by the neural networks found in the human brain. Autonomous vehicles and the Internet of Things are being revolutionized by neuromorphic processors.

- **Field-Programmable Gate Arrays (FPGAs):** These adaptable processors provide versatility in hybrid systems, enabling engineers to set them up for a variety of applications, such as cryptography and signal processing.

2.2 Technologies for Storage

Large volumes of data must be supported by storage solutions in hybrid computing systems that provide speed, scalability, and dependability. The complexities of hybrid storage technology are explored in this section.

Hybrid Storage Options: In-Memory Computing, HDDs, and SSDs

A variety of storage types are used by hybrid systems to balance capacity, performance, and cost:

- **Solid-State Drives (SSDs):** renowned for their durability and speed, SSDs are perfect for supporting real-time applications and gaining access to frequently utilized data.

- **HDDs (hard disk drives):** HDDs provide high-capacity, reasonably priced storage, which makes them appropriate for archiving applications in hybrid systems, even if they are slower than SSDs.

- **In-Memory Computing:** Using RAM for short-term data storage guarantees lightning-fast access and processing, which is essential for workloads involving AI, real-time analytics, and high-frequency trading.

Optimizing Data Access in Hybrid Environments

In hybrid settings, efficient data access techniques are essential to reducing latency and improving performance:

- **Caching Mechanisms:** To speed up retrieval, frequently accessed data is kept in faster storage layers like SSDs or RAM.

- **Data Tiering:** To ensure optimal performance and cost-effectiveness, hybrid systems dynamically distribute data between storage tiers according to consumption patterns.

- **Distributed File Systems:** Hadoop Distributed File

System (HDFS) and other technologies provide easy data replication and access in on-premises and hybrid cloud settings.

Aspects of Scalability in Storage

A key component of hybrid storage solutions is scalability, which enables systems to adjust to expanding data requirements:

- **Elastic Storage:** Without requiring actual hardware changes, cloud storage services offer on-demand scalability to accommodate varying workloads.

- **Hybrid Cloud Storage:** By combining cloud and local storage, hybrid systems give users the option to store non-essential data in the cloud and sensitive data on-site.

- **Object Storage:** Platforms such as Amazon S3 allow for scalable storage of unstructured data, which is becoming more and more prevalent in hybrid computing applications like big data analytics and media storage.

2.3 Hybrid System Networking

Strong networking is the foundation of hybrid computing, allowing for smooth component connectivity and guaranteeing effective data flow. The important elements of networking in hybrid systems are examined in this section.

Combining High-Speed and Conventional Networks

To link local and dispersed components, hybrid systems need a variety of networking solutions:

- **Conventional Networks:** Ethernet and Wi-Fi networks offer dependable connectivity for consumer devices and on-premise equipment.
- **High-Speed Networks:** 5G and fiber optic technologies allow for quick data transfer between hybrid systems, facilitating applications like cloud gaming and real-time video streaming.
- **Software-Defined Networking (SDN):** SDN enables hybrid systems to dynamically manage network resources, maximizing performance and reducing bottlenecks by separating control from hardware.

The Function of Edge Computing in Hybrid

Configurations

Edge computing is an essential part of hybrid systems since it lowers latency by processing data closer to its source:

- **Real-Time Processing:** Edge devices that evaluate data locally before synchronizing with central systems are useful for applications such as driverless cars and smart cities.

- **Decreased Bandwidth Usage:** Hybrid systems reduce the requirement for continuous data transport by carrying out calculations at the edge, which lowers expenses and improves efficiency.

- **Cloud Integration:** By managing local processing and shifting computationally demanding tasks to the cloud, edge computing easily integrates with cloud resources.

Management of Data Flow and Reduction of Latency

Effective data flow control guarantees that hybrid systems operate well in a variety of settings:

- **Load balancing:** By dividing up workloads among several systems, bottlenecks are avoided and resource usage is maximized.

- **Content Delivery Networks (CDNs):** In hybrid

configurations, CDNs lower latency for end users by caching data at geographically separated locations.

- **Latency Reduction Techniques:** In order to ensure that hybrid systems satisfy the requirements of time-sensitive applications, technologies such as network slicing and multi-path routing improve data transfer speeds.

The strong and flexible architecture of hybrid computing is based on its fundamental elements, which include networking, storage technologies, and computation algorithms. In order to meet the complicated needs of contemporary computing, hybrid systems include cutting-edge CPUs, scalable storage, and effective networking. Designing and executing hybrid solutions that spur innovation across industries requires an understanding of these elements.

CHAPTER 3

ARTIFICIAL INTELLIGENCE WITH HYBRID COMPUTING

The development of artificial intelligence (AI) now depends heavily on hybrid computing. The complex demands of AI workloads are met by hybrid systems, which integrate several processing paradigms and resources. From model training to large-scale inference and overcoming computational constraints, this chapter examines how hybrid computing improves AI.

3.1 Improving Training of AI Models

Training AI models is a resource-intensive procedure that frequently calls for a large amount of processing power and advanced data management. Hybrid computing uses cutting-edge architectures and customized hardware to enhance these operations.

GPU and TPU Combination for Effective Training

In order to effectively manage millions of parameters, AI model training particularly in deep learning requires parallel processing capability.

- **Graphics Processing Units (GPUs):** These devices are perfect for jobs like convolutional operations in neural networks since they are excellent at matrix operations and parallel processing.

- TPUs, or tensor processing units, are: TPUs, which were created especially for AI, offer tensor operations optimal performance, which is essential in machine learning frameworks such as TensorFlow.

- **Hybrid Synergy:** Hybrid systems provide quicker and more effective training by combining GPUs for general parallel workloads and TPUs for specialized tensor computations.

For instance, certain tasks are delegated to TPUs for training generative models such as GPTs or image recognition networks, while GPUs are responsible for data preprocessing and augmentation.

Hybrid Storage for Managing Large Datasets

AI model training necessitates the management of large

datasets that require reliable storage and fast access.

- **Tiered Storage:** While archive datasets are stored on HDDs or in cloud environments, hybrid systems use SSDs to retrieve data quickly during active training.

- **In-Memory Computing:** Training data that is frequently used is cached in memory, which significantly speeds up the process and reduces the amount of time needed to retrieve the data.

- **Scalability:** AI researchers can easily expand their datasets by including additional data sources without interfering with workflows thanks to hybrid storage.

The Role of Edge Computing in Real-Time AI Applications

Edge computing is essential for low-latency processing in real-time AI applications, including smart devices and driverless cars.

- **Localized Processing:** Hybrid systems ensure quick responses by processing data at the edge, eliminating the requirement for data transfer to centralized systems.

- **AI at the Edge:** The cloud manages model updates

and training, while tasks like anomaly detection and picture identification are carried out locally.

- **Energy Efficiency:** By doing calculations nearer the data source, edge computing lowers energy consumption, which is an important consideration in mobile and Internet of Things applications.

3.2 Scalable AI Inference

One of the most important phases in implementing AI systems is AI inference, which involves applying learned models to fresh data. When it comes to scaling inference procedures across multiple applications, hybrid computing is revolutionary.

Hybrid Systems for Quick AI Deduction

When AI models are deployed, real-time predictions are frequently made, necessitating quick and precise processing:

- **Distributed Inference:** To optimize efficiency, hybrid systems divide inference tasks among GPUs, CPUs, and edge devices.
- In order to prevent bottlenecks during periods of

high demand, dynamic resource allocation guarantees that computational resources are used as efficiently as possible.

- **Latency Reduction:** Hybrid configurations use edge computing and high-speed networking to reduce latency, which is crucial for applications like voice recognition and video analytics.

Deep Learning through the Integration of Neuromorphic Computing

A paradigm change in AI inference is brought about by neuromorphic computing, which efficiently processes information by imitating the neural architecture of the brain:

- **Spike-Based Models:** Spiking neural networks are handled by neuromorphic processors, allowing for energy-efficient inference for tasks like language translation and object detection.
- **Hybrid Implementation:** Hybrid architectures combine neuromorphic devices with conventional AI systems to provide improved performance and lower power consumption.
- Neuromorphic integration is useful in domains

where real-time processing and adaptive learning are critical, such as robots and healthcare.

The following real-world examples demonstrate the revolutionary effects of hybrid computing in AI:

Case Studies of AI Applications Leveraging Hybrid Computing

- **Healthcare:** By combining edge medical imaging equipment with cloud-based AI models, hybrid solutions allow for quick disease diagnosis.
- **Autonomous Vehicles:** AI-powered cars use cloud resources for system updates and route planning, and edge computing for real-time sensor data processing.
- **Retail and E-Commerce:** Recommendation engines are powered by hybrid AI systems that integrate on-device personalization with cloud-based analytics to provide smooth user experiences.

3.3 Dealing with the Computational Boundaries of AI

AI still has a lot of computational and scalability issues despite its progress. Solutions to push these limits and open up new possibilities are provided by hybrid computing.

Restrictions of Present-Day AI Technologies

AI models run into computational and resource availability limitations as their complexity increases:

- **Data Volume:** Conventional systems frequently become overwhelmed when handling large datasets during training and inference.
- **Energy Consumption:** Deep learning and other AI computations use a lot of energy, which raises environmental issues.
- **Latency:** In centralized computing settings, applications that need to make decisions instantly suffer from delays.

Hybrid Approaches to Expanding AI's Potential

Hybrid systems overcome AI's drawbacks and increase its potential by combining various computational resources:

- **Federated Learning:** By utilizing distributed resources and maintaining data privacy, hybrid configurations allow decentralized model training across numerous devices.
- **Dynamic Resource Allocation:** AI systems may

dynamically distribute workloads according to job requirements thanks to hybrid computing, which maximizes efficiency and speed.

- **Quantum Integration:** To address issues like protein folding and large-scale optimization, emerging hybrid systems integrate quantum computing with traditional AI techniques.

Prospects for AI-Powered Hybrid Computing in the Future

Technology landscapes are about to be redefined by the confluence of AI and hybrid computing:

- **AI-Powered Hybrid Clouds:** By automating workload distribution, intelligent resource management solutions will improve hybrid cloud performance.

- **Hyper-Personalization:** Real-time customization will be fueled by hybrid AI systems in industries including entertainment, healthcare, and education.

- **Sustainable AI:** The environmental impact of extensive AI deployments will be addressed via energy-efficient hybrid architectures that combine neuromorphic processors and edge computing.

- **Autonomous Systems:** By fusing real-time decision-making with sophisticated analytics, hybrid computing will power the next generation of autonomous technologies, from intelligent drones to self-driving cars.

By meeting artificial intelligence's computational requirements and opening up new creative possibilities, hybrid computing is transforming the field. Hybrid systems enable AI to address challenging real-world problems by improving model training, scaling inference, and getting past intrinsic constraints. An important step toward a more intelligent and effective technological future is the combination of hybrid computing with artificial intelligence.

CHAPTER 4

HYBRID COMPUTING APPLICATIONS

A key component in the advancement of numerous sectors is hybrid computing, which combines various processing paradigms and resources. New avenues for scientific research, healthcare, and financial services are made possible by hybrid computing, which tackles particular problems and offers scalable solutions. This chapter explores various uses and explains how they can be transformative.

4.1 Medical Care

Hybrid computing is revolutionizing the healthcare sector by advancing medical research, improving patient outcomes, and increasing operational efficiency.

Precision Medicine and Hybrid Computing

Precision medicine uses lifestyle, environmental, and

genetic data to customize treatment regimens for each patient. In order to analyze and interpret the large datasets needed for these endeavors, hybrid computing is essential.

- **Genomic Data Analysis:** By combining cloud platforms and high-performance computing (HPC), hybrid systems are able to analyze genomic data and find mutations and biomarkers on a never-before-seen scale.

- **Machine Learning Models:** By fusing classical computers for statistical analysis with GPU-accelerated deep learning, sophisticated hybrid AI systems forecast treatment outcomes.

- **Interoperability:** Hybrid computing guarantees smooth access to patient data across institutions by connecting on-premises analytical tools with cloud-based databases.

Real-Time Analysis of Medical Imaging

Medical imaging produces massive datasets that need to be processed quickly in order to diagnose and plan treatments.

- **Edge Computing:** In crucial situations, hybrid systems handle imaging data, including CT and MRI images, at the edge for real-time analysis.

- **Cloud Collaboration:** Telemedicine consultations and collaborative diagnosis are made possible by remote professionals having access to high-resolution images processed by hybrid cloud systems.

- **AI Integration:** By detecting abnormalities like tumors or fractures, hybrid AI models improve diagnostic precision and cut down on the amount of time needed for manual evaluation.

Securely Managing Patient Data

Healthcare institutions are required to adhere to stringent data privacy laws while managing sensitive patient data.

- **Hybrid Cloud Storage:** Cloud systems are used for large-scale analytics, but patient data is kept on-site for increased protection.

- **Encryption and Access Control:** By utilizing multi-layered security, hybrid systems guarantee that patient records are only accessible by authorized individuals.

- **Disaster Recovery:** Hybrid architectures guarantee continuity of treatment by enabling safe backups and quick patient data recovery in an emergency.

4.2 Financial Services

In order to manage enormous volumes of data, streamline decision-making procedures, and reduce risks, the financial industry is depending more and more on hybrid computing.

Risk Analysis Using Hybrid Computing

Financial firms evaluate the risks of loans, investments, and market swings using hybrid systems.

- **Monte Carlo Simulations:** By dividing up calculations between CPUs and GPUs, hybrid computing makes it possible to execute complex risk models more quickly.
- **Real-Time Monitoring:** Edge computing makes it easier to analyze market trends in real time, which guarantees prompt decision-making.
- **Predictive Analytics:** AI-powered hybrid systems estimate market dangers and opportunities by analyzing real-time and historical data.

Speeding Up Algorithmic Trading

Algorithmic trading uses quick calculations to carry out

deals according to preset strategies.

- **Low-Latency Networks:** To reduce trade execution delays, hybrid systems combine edge computing and high-speed networking.
- **Parallel Processing:** By speeding up the execution of intricate algorithms, GPUs allow traders to react to market movements in milliseconds.
- **Data Integration:** By combining data from international marketplaces, hybrid cloud platforms give traders thorough insights for optimizing their strategies.

Improving Fraud Detection

Real-time analysis of massive amounts of data is necessary to identify fraudulent activity in financial transactions.

- Hybrid AI systems identify irregularities in transaction patterns and highlight possible fraud for additional examination using Machine Learning Models.
- **Distributed Processing:** Hybrid architectures ensure scalability and speed in fraud detection by analyzing data across several nodes.
- **Cross-Border Collaboration:** Hybrid technologies

help financial institutions share data securely, bolstering international efforts to fight fraud.

4.3 Research in Science

Hybrid computing greatly aids scientific research by allowing researchers to effectively evaluate large datasets and solve computationally demanding challenges.

Modeling and Simulation in Hybrid Environments

- From astrophysical phenomena to molecular interactions, hybrid computing is essential for simulating complex systems.
- **HPC and Cloud Integration:** Researchers may simulate scenarios at a never-before-seen scale by combining cloud resources with HPC clusters.
- **Parallel Computation:** CPUs orchestrate data, while GPUs do complex computations, including fluid dynamics simulations.
- **Visualization Tools:** To help with data interpretation and presentation, hybrid systems produce high-resolution visuals of simulation findings.

Increasing Genomic Examination

Genomic research is computationally intensive and focuses on understanding genetic features and diseases by studying DNA sequences.

- **Hybrid Pipelines:** While large-scale sequence alignment and analysis are carried out on cloud platforms, data preprocessing takes place on local servers.

- **AI-Powered Insights:** Targeted therapy development is accelerated by hybrid systems that employ AI models to find gene variations associated with diseases.

- **Collaboration Platforms**: Researchers from all across the world work together in hybrid settings, exchanging tools and data to make genetic discoveries.

In order to support large-scale climate investigations, it is necessary to handle enormous datasets from environmental sensors, weather stations, and satellites.

- **Data Fusion:** For thorough climate modeling, hybrid systems combine several data sources, including satellite imagery and oceanic observations.

- **Real-Time Analysis:** Edge computing makes it possible to track environmental changes in real time, which helps with disaster reaction and preparation.
- **Predictive Modeling:** Hybrid AI models predict climate changes, offering information for resource management and government.

The disruptive potential of hybrid computing is demonstrated by its applications in scientific research, healthcare, and financial services. Through the integration of many computational paradigms, hybrid systems facilitate innovative scientific discoveries, optimize financial processes, and enable precision medicine. Hybrid computing's influence will only increase as more industries adopt it, spurring innovation and tackling global issues.

CHAPTER 5

Hybrid Computing Difficulties

By combining several computational paradigms, hybrid computing has enormous potential, but implementing it is fraught with difficulties. Unlocking the full potential of hybrid systems requires addressing these issues. The main integration, cost, and security barriers are examined in this chapter along with their ramifications and mitigating techniques.

5.1 Complexity of Integration

The foundation of hybrid computing is the smooth integration of several systems, which frequently calls for complex coordination between the network, software, and hardware levels.

Combining Various Computing Paradigms

Conventional CPUs, GPUs, and specialist processors like

TPUs and FPGAs are all integrated into hybrid systems. The variety of these paradigms makes it difficult to provide the best possible compatibility and performance.

- **Heterogeneous Architectures:** To manage resource allocation and unify workloads, combining these disparate architectures calls for complex middleware and frameworks.

- The process of workload partitioning: It can be difficult to determine which activities should be performed on which component because some paradigms perform different kinds of calculations better than others.

- **Standardization:** Organizations are forced to rely on proprietary solutions due to the complexity of the integration process caused by the absence of widely recognized standards.

Synchronization Issues in Hybrid Setups

Another significant challenge is making sure that every part of a hybrid system functions as a whole.

- **Latency Mismatches:** Processing processes are hampered by the disparity in speed between GPUs, CPUs, and storage systems.

- **Data Consistency:** Particularly in real-time applications, synchronizing data across dispersed systems may cause delays or discrepancies.

- **Orchestration Challenges:** To prioritize work across several nodes and handle dependencies, effective orchestration tools are required.

Overcoming Software Compatibility Challenges

When merging several platforms and applications, software compatibility problems can occur.

- **Driver and API Support:** In order to facilitate communication between components, hybrid systems frequently need updated drivers and APIs.

- **Legacy Systems:** Compatibility and performance problems may arise when integrating older technologies into a contemporary hybrid framework.

- **Development Complexity:** Writing software that fully utilizes hybrid computing necessitates specific knowledge and equipment, which makes development cycles more complicated.

5.2 Expense Factors

Significant upfront and ongoing financial investments are linked to hybrid computing. For broad adoption, cost issues must be resolved.

High Initial Infrastructure Investment

A variety of hardware and software components must be purchased and configured in order to set up a hybrid computing system.

- **Specialized Hardware:** The deployment of GPUs, TPUs, and edge devices can put a strain on budgets due to their high cost.

- **Infrastructure Upgrades:** To enable hybrid functionality, such as improved networking and storage capacities, existing systems may need to be upgraded.

- **Personnel Costs:** The initial costs are increased when qualified experts are hired for system setup, maintenance, and optimization.

Equating Performance Benefits with Costs

Businesses frequently find it difficult to defend the costs of hybrid computing against the expected performance improvements.

- **Assigning Resources:** Avoiding wasteful spending can be achieved by determining which workloads actually benefit from hybrid systems.

- **Efficiency versus Performance:** Energy-intensive high-performance systems can eventually raise operating expenses.

- **ROI Analysis:** Performing comprehensive cost-benefit analysis guarantees that investments meet company objectives and yield measurable results.

Cost-Effective Hybrid Implementation Strategies

Strategic planning can help allay financial worries while preserving hybrid computing's benefits.

- **Cloud Utilization:** By using cloud services for some system components, a large amount of on-premises hardware is not required.

- **Open-Source Solutions:** Using open-source frameworks and tools reduces licensing costs.

- **Incremental Deployment:** By integrating hybrid systems gradually, businesses can spread out expenses over time and acquire technological expertise.

5.3 Security Issues

Strong security measures are required to secure sensitive data and guarantee system integrity since hybrid computing poses special threats.

Hybrid System Vulnerabilities

Multiple points of vulnerability are created by the distributed nature of hybrid systems.

- **Attack Surfaces:** Every part, from cloud servers to edge devices, offers possible points of entry for cyberattacks.
- **Data Interception:** In hybrid configurations, data sent across networks is vulnerable to modification and interception.
- **Internal Dangers:** Multiple stakeholders are frequently involved in hybrid setups, which raises the possibility of internal illegal access.

Safeguarding Data in Hybrid Environments

Because hybrid computing handles sensitive data, data protection is a primary concern.

- **Encryption:** Using end-to-end encryption guarantees that data is safe both during storage and transmission.

- Only authorized personnel are able to access data thanks to role-based access control measures.

- Segmenting the data: The impact of such breaches is lessened by dividing sensitive material into smaller, more manageable sections.

Strong security measures should be put in place to assist reduce risks and guarantee the security of hybrid systems.

- **Continuous Audits:** Finding vulnerabilities and ensuring adherence to best practices are two benefits of conducting regular security assessments.

- Advanced Threat Detection: AI-powered security solutions keep an eye on hybrid settings in real time, spotting and thwarting possible dangers.

- The implementation of thorough disaster recovery procedures guarantees data accessibility and system continuity in the event of a breach.

Despite being revolutionary, hybrid computing has drawbacks. Organizations must overcome many obstacles to realize its full potential, including the difficulties of integration, the costs of deployment, and the crucial requirement for strong security. Businesses and researchers can use hybrid computing to foster innovation and accomplish their goals by comprehending these issues and putting strategic solutions in place.

CHAPTER 6

HYBRID SYSTEMS USING QUANTUM AND OPTICAL COMPUTING

New levels of processing power and efficiency have been made possible by the merging of cutting-edge paradigms like quantum and optical computing as hybrid computing develops. The function of quantum and optical computing in hybrid systems, their distinct advantages, and the difficulties of fusing these ground-breaking technologies are all covered in this chapter.

6.1 Quantum Computing's Role

For some issue types, quantum computing offers exponential speedups by introducing a fundamentally new method of information processing. By incorporating it into hybrid systems, previously unsolvable issues are resolved and computational capability is increased.

The Principles of Quantum Computing: An Introduction

In order to process data, quantum computing makes use of concepts like superposition, entanglement, and quantum interference.

- **Qubits:** Parallel processing is made possible by qubits' ability to exist in several states at once, in contrast to traditional bits that can only hold values of 0 or 1.

- **Quantum Gates:** Quantum gates, which modify probabilities and establish extremely effective computing paths, are used to carry out operations on qubits.

- **Quantum Advantage:** Quantum algorithms like Shor's or Grover's are orders of magnitude faster at some jobs, including factoring big numbers or optimizing complicated systems.

The term "hybrid quantum-classical models" refers to systems in which quantum computing complements classical computing rather than replacing it.

- **Task Allocation:** Quantum systems take on computationally demanding jobs, whereas classical systems manage data pre-processing and error correction.

- **Middleware Integration:** Communication between quantum and classical systems is facilitated by quantum-specific software layers and APIs such as Qiskit or Cirq.

- **Iterative Computation:** Using both classical accuracy and quantum speed, hybrid models iteratively improve findings.

Quantum computing applications in hybrid environments

Applications for quantum computing in hybrid systems can be found in a variety of fields:

- **Cryptography:** Conventional encryption techniques are broken by quantum algorithms, which improve secure communications.

- **Optimization:** Quantum systems are used in sectors such as banking and logistics to solve intricate optimization issues.

- **Scientific Research:** By simulating molecular interactions at previously unheard-of scales, quantum simulations speed up material science and drug development.

6.2 Integration of Optical Computing

Utilizing photons instead of electrons, optical computing enhances both conventional and quantum computing paradigms by providing hybrid systems with unparalleled speed and energy efficiency.

Basics of Optical Computing

Light-based technologies like lasers and photonic circuits are used in optical computing to process information.

- **Photonics:** Data is encoded and sent by using the wavelength and amplitude of light.
- **Optical Logic Gates:** These gates use light signals to facilitate fast computations.
- **Wave Interference:** To conduct complicated operations effectively, optical systems take advantage of wave interference.

The benefits of optical computing over electronic computing

- Because of its many benefits, optical computing is a

useful complement to hybrid systems.

- Because light moves more quickly than electrons, data can be processed and transmitted more quickly.

- Bandwidth: Because optical systems can encode data in various wavelengths, they can accommodate larger data densities.

- Energy Efficiency: Compared to conventional electronics, optical systems are more environmentally friendly due to their lower power and heat generation.

Optical Technologies Utilized by Hybrid Systems

Adding optical computing to hybrid systems expands their potential:

- **Data Centers**: Optical interconnects decrease bottlenecks in large-scale computations and increase data transfer speeds.

- **AI and Machine Learning:** A key element of AI algorithms, matrix computations, are accelerated by optical processors.

- **Real-Time Applications:** The almost instantaneous response times of optical systems are advantageous to sectors such as financial trading and telecommunications.

6.3 Integrating Optical and Quantum Systems

Although hybrid systems that combine quantum and optical computing offer a paradigm change in computer technology, they also pose special difficulties.

Optical and Quantum Computing Synergies

The complementary nature of quantum and optical computing technologies increases the overall effectiveness of hybrid systems:

- **Quantum Photonics:** By decreasing decoherence and boosting scalability, photonic qubits enable quantum calculations.
- Fast Quantum Gate Operations: Optical devices improve processing throughput by enabling faster quantum gate implementations.
- **Improved Error Rates:** By reducing errors in quantum systems, optical approaches provide more dependable results.

Difficulties with Integration

It is difficult to integrate optical and quantum systems into a single hybrid environment:

- Because quantum and optical systems function on separate physical principles, they require sophisticated interface technology. This is known as hardware compatibility.

- **Stability and Scalability:** It is difficult to keep quantum systems coherent and to guarantee steady performance in optical systems.

- **Expensive Prices:** Large financial and technical investments are required for the development and implementation of hybrid quantum-optical systems.

Practical Use Cases

Successful applications of quantum and optical hybrid systems show their revolutionary potential in spite of the difficulties:

- **Quantum Communication Networks:** Secure long-distance dissemination of quantum keys is made possible by optical technologies.

- **Advanced Cryptography:** Hybrid quantum-optical systems provide previously unheard-of security levels for private information.

- **Science-Based Models:** These systems are used by researchers to model intricate biological processes and quantum field interactions.

As parts of hybrid systems, quantum and optical computing push the limits of computational capability. Hybrid systems can handle difficult problems in a variety of fields, including scientific research and cryptography, by utilizing the advantages of various paradigms. But in order to reach their full potential, major integration and financial obstacles must be resolved. Quantum-optical hybrid systems have the potential to completely transform computing in the future with further development.

CHAPTER 7

CREATING SYSTEMS FOR HYBRID COMPUTING

The process of creating hybrid computing systems is intricate and calls for meticulous design, the use of state-of-the-art tools, and ongoing optimization. The main design concepts, frameworks and tools, and testing techniques necessary for building reliable and effective hybrid computing systems are examined in this chapter.

7.1 Design Guidelines

Strategic planning is required to balance a number of trade-offs while achieving performance objectives while designing a hybrid computing system.

Important Things to Think About When Developing Hybrid Systems

Understanding the operational limitations and computational requirements is the first step in creating a hybrid system:

- **Workload Analysis:** Determine whether workloads are real-time, data-intensive, or compute-intensive in order to deploy resources efficiently.

- **Hardware Integration:** To optimize computing efficiency, combine CPUs, GPUs, and specialized processors like FPGAs or TPUs.

- **Data Management:** Put in place hybrid storage options that provide easy access to data in dispersed settings.

Balancing Scalability, Cost, and Performance

Hybrid systems need to balance cost-effectiveness, scalability, and high performance:

- **Performance:** Build the system to minimize latency and effectively manage heavy workloads.

- As computing demands increase, make sure the architecture can scale without requiring major redesigns.

- **Cost Management:** To cut down on operating costs, make the most of both on-premises and cloud resources.

- For non-essential tasks, use spot instances on the

cloud.

- Use auto-scaling mechanisms to make dynamic adjustments to resource allocation.

The function of software in the design of hybrid systems

For hybrid hardware to function smoothly and reach its full potential, the software stack is essential:

- The use of middleware to bridge the gap between various hardware components and application software is known as middleware solutions.

- **Tools for Orchestration:** Workload management and effective resource use are ensured by tools such as Kubernetes.

- **Personalized Algorithms:** Create algorithms specifically for hybrid architectures to improve performance.

7.2 Frameworks and Tools

To make the construction and administration of hybrid computing systems more efficient, a range of tools and frameworks are available.

Popular Hybrid Computing Tools: A few tools have proved indispensable in the field of hybrid computing:

- One tool for container orchestration that effectively manages hybrid cloud settings is called Kubernetes.
- A unified analytics engine for analyzing huge amounts of data, Apache Spark is frequently utilized in hybrid environments.
- Two machine learning frameworks that facilitate hybrid computing spanning CPUs, GPUs, and TPUs are TensorFlow and PyTorch.

New Frameworks and How They Are Used

New frameworks are being developed as hybrid computing advances to meet certain issues:

- A distributed computing architecture called Ray is perfect for growing AI and ML applications in mixed environments.
- Dask is a versatile Python module for parallel computing that is helpful for applications involving a lot of data.
- An open-source cloud operating system called OpenStack makes it easier to manage hybrid cloud infrastructure.

Open-Source Hybrid Environment Solutions

Open-source tools offer hybrid computing alternatives that are both affordable and adaptable:

- One scalable storage option that works well with hybrid systems is Ceph.
- Prometheus is a monitoring system that assists with troubleshooting and tracks performance data.
- Ansible is an automation tool that makes deployment and configuration of hybrid systems easier.

7.3 Optimization and Testing

For hybrid computing systems to operate dependably and effectively, extensive testing and ongoing optimization are essential.

Performance Evaluation in Hybrid Configurations

Assessing both software and hardware components is part of testing hybrid systems:

- **Load Testing:** To evaluate system resilience and locate bottlenecks, simulate peak loads.
- **Latency Measurement:** To guarantee smooth data

flow, examine reaction times at various nodes.

- **Tests for Scalability:** Check to see if the system can manage higher workloads without experiencing a drop in performance.

Methods for Hybrid System Optimization

Optimizing hybrid systems guarantees optimal performance:

- Utilize clever schedulers to dynamically distribute resources according to workload demands.
- **Data Compression:** To cut down on latency and bandwidth consumption, reduce the amount of data that is sent between components.
- **Energy Efficiency:** Reduce operating expenses by implementing power-aware computing techniques.

As an illustration, Dynamic Voltage and Frequency Scaling (DVFS) modifies processor speeds in response to the severity of the task.

Ongoing Observation for Enhancement

Continuous monitoring is necessary for hybrid systems in order to detect and resolve performance problems:

- **Systems of Telemetry:** To get up-to-date

information on system performance and resource utilization, use telemetry.

- **Predictive Analytics:** Make use of AI-driven technologies to anticipate possible malfunctions and take preventative measures.
- **Continuous Updates:** To take advantage of the most recent developments, keep both hardware and software components updated.

The creation of hybrid computing systems is a science and an art. Organizations can develop systems that are strong and flexible by following fundamental design principles, utilizing state-of-the-art tools and frameworks, and dedicating themselves to thorough testing and optimization. These procedures will continue to be essential to maximizing the potential of hybrid computing as it develops further.

CHAPTER 8

HYBRID COMPUTING'S FUTURE TRENDS

Technology advancements and the growing complexity of computing requirements are driving the ongoing evolution of the hybrid computing landscape. With an emphasis on neuromorphic computing, edge computing developments, and the changing paradigms defining the next generation of hybrid systems, this chapter examines the major trends that will influence hybrid computing in the future.

8.1 Neuromorphic Computing's Development

By simulating the neuronal architecture of the human brain, the innovative discipline of neuromorphic computing makes computing more intelligent and efficient.

An Overview of Neuromorphic Technology

The architecture and operation of biological brain networks serve as models for neuromorphic computing:

- It makes use of spiking neural networks (SNNs), which process data similarly to how synapses in the brain do their function.

- Neuromorphic processors, like IBM's TrueNorth and Intel's Loihi, prioritize real-time computing and power efficiency.

- Neuromorphic systems perform exceptionally well on tasks involving pattern recognition, decision-making, and sensory data processing, in contrast to conventional computers.

Complementing Hybrid Systems

The integration of neuromorphic technologies into hybrid systems has enormous promise.

- **Enhanced AI Training:** By enhancing neural network training efficiency, neuromorphic devices can be used in conjunction with GPUs and TPUs.

- **Edge Deployment:** Because neuromorphic chips use very little energy, they are perfect for edge devices in hybrid systems.

- **Apps in Real Time**: Use cases that demand low latency and high adaptability include Internet of Things (IoT) devices, robotics, and driverless cars.

Future Uses in AI and Other Fields

Neuromorphic computing's potential to revolutionize how hybrid systems approach challenging problems is what will determine its future:

- **Personalized AI:** Real-time adaptation to user behavior is possible with devices that include on-chip learning capabilities.
- **Cognitive Systems:** These systems are capable of simulating human-like reasoning in order to solve complex problems.
- **Energy Efficiency Revolution:** In hybrid data centers, neuromorphic computing can dramatically lower energy usage.

8.2 Edge Computing Developments

Faster data processing near the source is made possible by edge computing, which has become a disruptive factor in hybrid systems.

The function of the edge in hybrid computing

A key component of contemporary hybrid architectures,

edge computing offers localized processing to support centralized cloud computing:

- **Latency Reduction:** Edge computing reduces latency by processing data close to the source, improving the responsiveness of applications like smart cities and driverless cars.

- **Bandwidth Optimization:** By eliminating the need to send massive amounts of data to the cloud, edge devices ease network congestion.

- **Privacy of Data:** Local processing of sensitive data enhances adherence to data protection laws.

Combining Cloud and Edge for Maximum Efficiency

In order to create reliable hybrid systems, edge and cloud computing must work together:

- **Dynamic Workload Distribution:** Depending on latency and computational demands, systems can distribute jobs to the cloud or the edge.

- **Cloud Backup:** To ensure durability and accessibility, the cloud offers a scalable and secure store for edge-generated data.

- **Real-Time Analytics:** While the cloud enables more in-depth, long-term analysis, edge computing provides instant insights.

Trends Fueling Adoption of the Edge

The use of edge computing in hybrid systems is being accelerated by a number of market and technological factors:

- **5G Networks:** Ultra-low latency is made possible by 5G, which is essential for edge deployments.
- **AI-Driven Edge:** More and more edge-based AI models are being used for applications like predictive maintenance and facial recognition.
- **IoT Proliferation:** Decentralized processing is necessary for the billions of connected devices in the expanding IoT ecosystem.

8.3 Changing Frameworks

Emerging breakthroughs and evolving requirements will promote a paradigm shift in hybrid computing systems as technology advances.

The Impact of Emerging Technologies on Hybrid Computing

A number of innovative technologies have the potential to completely transform hybrid systems:

- **Quantum Computing:** As quantum systems become more widely available, they will be incorporated into hybrid designs to address particular issues like optimization and cryptography.

- **Photonic Computing:** It is anticipated that optical technology will overcome the speed and bandwidth constraints of electronic computing.

- **Distributed Ledger Technology (DLT):** DLT, which includes blockchain, can improve transparency and security in hybrid settings.

Incorporation of Next-Generation Processors

As processor technology develops, it provides hybrid systems with previously unheard-of capabilities:

- The use of energy-efficient ARM processors in hybrid systems is growing, particularly for edge and mobile computing.

- **Heterogeneous Computing Units (HCUs):** These optimize performance across a range of workloads by combining disparate processing components into a single framework.

- **Chips with Built-In AI Capabilities:** AI accelerators in processors allow machine learning operations to be executed more quickly on hardware.

Suggestions for the Upcoming Decade

Hybrid computing is expected to undergo significant change during the next ten years:

- **Ubiquitous Hybrid Systems:** Hybrid architectures will proliferate across industries, enabling everything from automated manufacturing to smart healthcare.

- **Technological Convergence:** By combining quantum, neuromorphic, and optical computing, the possibilities of hybrid systems will be expanded.

- **Autonomous Systems:** As robotics and AI improve, hybrid systems will make it possible for fully autonomous operations in sectors like agriculture and logistics.

- **Sustainability Focus:** Data centers powered by renewable energy sources and energy-efficient designs will proliferate, making hybrid systems more ecologically benign.

Hybrid computing's future represents an exciting fusion of creativity and usefulness. While edge computing reimagines real-time capabilities, neuromorphic computing provides a window into intelligent and effective processing. Hybrid computing is set to spearhead the next ten years of technological developments as changing paradigms incorporate new technologies and next-generation processors. In addition to promising revolutionary applications, these developments emphasize the need for sustainable and adaptable computing solutions in a world that is constantly evolving.

CHAPTER 9

INDUSTRY 4.0 AND HYBRID COMPUTING

The advent of Industry 4.0 heralds a revolutionary period in which physical systems and digital technology coexist harmoniously to construct intelligent, networked ecosystems. This change is mostly being driven by hybrid computing, which combines the best aspects of several computer paradigms. This chapter explores how hybrid computing contributes to Industry 4.0 cybersecurity, smart manufacturing, and the Internet of Things (IoT).

9.1 Intelligent Production

The core of Industry 4.0, which is defined by the integration of automation, data interchange, and advanced analytics, is smart manufacturing. By fusing the advantages of cloud, edge, and specialized computing systems, hybrid computing improves these capabilities.

Hybrid Systems' Function in Automation

Manufacturing automation necessitates reliable and flexible systems:

- **Process Optimization**: Hybrid systems allow for real-time manufacturing process monitoring and modification, reducing waste and increasing productivity.

- **Collaborative Robots (Cobots):** Cobots improve safety and efficiency by interacting with human operators in a seamless manner through the use of hybrid computing.

- **Predictive Maintenance**: Hybrid systems anticipate and avoid machinery problems, minimizing downtime, by evaluating equipment performance data in real-time.

Analytics in Real Time in Production Settings

Real-time analysis of enormous volumes of industrial data is revolutionary:

- **Edge Computing for Instant Insights**: By processing vital data at the edge, hybrid systems allow for immediate reactions to irregularities.

- **Cloud-Enhanced Analysis:** Long-term insights and

optimization methods are obtained by analyzing data pooled from many facilities in the cloud.

- **AI-Powered Decision-Making:** AI models that operate on hybrid systems find inefficiencies, suggest fixes, and guarantee the best possible use of available resources.

Improving Operational Efficiency

Hybrid computing has a major role in simplifying manufacturing processes:

- **Energy Management:** Smart systems help achieve sustainability goals by optimizing energy consumption throughout production lines.

- **Supply Chain Integration:** Hybrid platforms enable real-time connections between distributors, manufacturers, and suppliers, enabling end-to-end visibility.

- **Custom Manufacturing:** Hybrid systems facilitate adaptable manufacturing procedures, allowing for prompt modifications to satisfy particular client needs.

9.2 Internet of Things (IoT)

With billions of linked devices producing an unprecedented volume of data, the Internet of Things is a key component of Industry 4.0. The infrastructure required to efficiently handle and process this data is offered by hybrid computing.

IoT's Dependency on Hybrid Computing

In order for IoT ecosystems to function smoothly, hybrid computing is necessary:

- **Distributed Processing:** Local computations are handled by edge devices, and when more processing power is required, it is supplied by the cloud.
- Hybrid systems guarantee consistent data integration and analysis across a variety of IoT devices, resulting in unified data management.
- **AI at the Edge:** AI models operate on edge devices with hybrid computing, allowing IoT apps to make decisions on their own.

Overseeing extensive IoT deployments

IoT network scaling has particular difficulties that hybrid

systems are well-suited to handle:

- **Efficient Data Handling:** Only pertinent data is sent to the cloud using hybrid systems, which filter and prioritize data at the edge.
- The ability to scale resources up or down in response to demand is made possible by cloud components of hybrid systems.
- **Interoperability:** Hybrid platforms facilitate smooth communication and coordination by integrating a variety of IoT devices.

Facilitating Instantaneous Internet of Things Applications

Real-time responsiveness is essential for many IoT applications, and hybrid computing is excellent at providing it:

- **Smart Cities:** The instantaneous processing capabilities of hybrid systems are advantageous for applications like public safety, energy distribution, and traffic control.
- **Healthcare IoT:** Hybrid computing improves patient care by enabling real-time monitoring and alarms for linked medical equipment.

- **Industrial IoT (IIoT)**: Smart grids, automated supply chains, and predictive maintenance are just a few of the industrial applications that are powered by hybrid systems.

9.3 Industry 4.0 Cybersecurity

The adoption of networked technologies in Industry 4.0 raises serious concerns about cybersecurity. Innovative ways to protect industrial environments from changing dangers are provided by hybrid computing.

Protecting Hybrid Systems in Industrial Environments

Specialized security procedures are necessary due to the particular vulnerabilities introduced by hybrid computing environments:

- Multi Layered Defense: To safeguard data at every level, hybrid systems use a mix of edge, cloud, and on-premises security mechanisms.
- **Encrypted Communication:** Advanced encryption algorithms are used to safeguard data transmission between components.
- Only authorized individuals can interact with vital

systems thanks to role-based access control.

Advanced Threat Detection with Hybrid AI

A key component of hybrid cybersecurity strategies is AI-powered threat detection:

- **Anomaly Detection:** Real-time flagging of possible breaches is facilitated by machine learning algorithms that detect anomalous patterns in system behavior.

- **Behavioral Analytics:** AI uses system and user behavior analysis to anticipate and neutralize risks before they materialize.

- **Rapid Response:** Hybrid systems minimize harm by enabling immediate containment and cleanup of cyber incidents.

Constructing Hybrid Infrastructures That Are Resilient

In industrial settings, resilience is essential to guaranteeing the dependability of hybrid systems:

- **Redundancy and Backup**: In the event of a failure, hybrid systems keep redundant components to guarantee continuous functioning.

- **Incident Recovery:** After interruptions, automated recovery systems quickly return to normal operations.

- **Continuous Monitoring:** To keep an eye out for vulnerabilities and preserve system integrity, hybrid systems make use of analytics and artificial intelligence.

Industry 4.0 is made possible in large part by hybrid computing, which offers the flexibility and processing capacity needed for cybersecurity, IoT, and smart manufacturing. Hybrid computing promotes creativity, effectiveness, and resilience by bridging the gap between digital and physical systems. The role of hybrid computing will grow as Industry 4.0 develops further, opening up new avenues and changing industrial operations globally.

CHAPTER 10

TRAINING AND EDUCATION WITH HYBRID COMPUTING

In addition to changing entire sectors, hybrid computing is also transforming worker training and education. Learning experiences are becoming more dynamic and impactful because of hybrid systems, which combine the power of many computing paradigms. This chapter examines how hybrid computing promotes cooperative research and development, improves STEM education, and equips professionals for new jobs.

10.1 Improving Education in STEM

At the vanguard of technological progress are the disciplines of science, technology, engineering, and mathematics, or STEM. In order to give students the skills and information they need to succeed in various fields, hybrid computing is essential.

Hybrid Computing's Function in Computational

Education

To provide a more engaging and useful learning environment, hybrid computing combines cutting-edge computational technologies with conventional teaching techniques:

- **Simulations and Modeling:** Students have hands-on experience with state-of-the-art technology by simulating complicated physical phenomena, such as protein folding and climate models, using hybrid systems.

- **Data-Driven Learning:** Students can examine big datasets and get valuable insights by using cloud-based datasets and edge computing platforms.

- **AI and Machine Learning:** Students may build, train, and implement machine learning models in practical settings thanks to hybrid computing, which enables AI courses.

Hybrid Learning Tools and Platforms

Hybrid computing in education is made possible by a variety of platforms and tools:

- **Cloud-Based Learning Platforms:** Computational resources for data analysis, simulations, and coding are accessible through services like Microsoft Azure and Google Cloud.

- **Virtual Labs:** Students can conduct experiments in virtual settings using platforms like Labster, which eliminates the need for tangible materials.
- **Edge Devices:** Students can experience computing at the edge through hands-on activities with Raspberry Pi and other inexpensive edge devices.

Using Hybrid Systems to Solve Real-World Issues

Students that use hybrid computing are better prepared to handle problems in the real world:

- **Interdisciplinary Projects:** Students work together across disciplines to find solutions in fields including energy, transportation, and healthcare by utilizing hybrid computing.
- Hybrid systems serve as the computational foundation for coding competitions and hackathons, encouraging creativity and innovation.
- **Capstone Projects:** To bridge the gap between academic learning and industrial demands, final-year students employ hybrid computing to solve real-world challenges.

10.2 Training of the Workforce

Workforce training programs must change to equip professionals for these new responsibilities as hybrid computing becomes more and more integrated into contemporary industry.

Educating Experts for Positions in Hybrid Computing

There is an increasing need for qualified experts who can plan, execute, and oversee hybrid systems:

- **Specialized Training Programs:** Training facilities and universities provide courses specifically designed for hybrid computing, emphasizing both theoretical understanding and hands-on abilities.

- **On-the-Job Training**: Businesses incorporate hybrid computing tools into their processes to give workers practical experience.

- **Learning by Doing:** Experts are urged to construct prototypes, test hybrid systems, and resolve problems unique to their sector.

Certification Programs and Resources

Certification programs improve professional opportunities by validating knowledge in hybrid computing:

- **Vendor-Specific Certifications**: Businesses such as Google, Microsoft, and AWS provide certifications in computing and hybrid cloud solutions.

- **General Certifications:** Organizations such as IEEE and CompTIA offer courses that concentrate on the principles and uses of hybrid systems.

- **Online Learning Platforms**: Coursera and Udemy, two platforms that frequently collaborate with leading companies in the field, provide hybrid computing courses.

Closing the Skills Gap in Emerging Technologies:
Training employees helps close the widening skills gap in hybrid computing.

- Through focused training programs, workers in conventional IT professions undergo reskilling and upskilling as they move to hybrid computing.

- **Mentorship and Peer Learning:** Newcomers are mentored by seasoned professionals, creating a cooperative learning atmosphere.

- **Accessible Education:** Training in hybrid

computing is now available to a worldwide audience through online courses and modular programs.

10.3 Research and Development in Collaboration

For hybrid computing technology to advance, industry and academia must work together. Collaborative research generates chances for shared learning and encourages innovation.

Hybrid Computing for Academic Research

To tackle intricate issues requiring a vast amount of processing power, researchers use hybrid systems:

- **Big Data Analysis:** In domains such as social sciences, astronomy, and genomics, hybrid systems handle and examine enormous datasets.

- **AI-Driven Discoveries:** Academic institutions create AI models for anything from drug discovery to climate modeling using hybrid computing.

- **Open Science Initiatives:** Researchers can work together across universities and exchange data thanks to hybrid platforms, which speeds up scientific discoveries.

Industry-Academia Partnerships

Industry-academia cooperation guarantees that research on hybrid computing stays relevant and useful:

- **Sponsored Research Projects:** Businesses provide funding for scholarly studies that investigate novel uses of hybrid computing.

- **Internship Programs:** Students apply their knowledge of hybrid computing to real-world situations while gaining practical experience in industry settings.

- **Collaborative Centers of Excellence**: Organizations and businesses set up specialized laboratories to develop hybrid computing technologies.

Inspiring Innovation Through Collaboration

Hybrid computing fosters innovation by dismantling disciplinary boundaries:

- **Cross-Disciplinary Teams:** Engineers and researchers from several disciplines work together to address challenging problems.

- **Open Source Contributions:** Projects involving

hybrid computing frequently support open-source communities, encouraging international cooperation.

- **businesses and Spin-Offs:** Commercial innovation is often fueled by hybrid computing research, which often results in the establishment of businesses.

Hybrid computing is revolutionizing workforce training and education by equipping professionals and students to meet the needs of a quickly changing technology environment. Its significance in influencing the direction of learning and innovation is highlighted by its contributions to improving STEM education, closing the skills gap, and encouraging collaborative research. Institutions and businesses alike can develop a generation capable of advancing society and addressing tomorrow's problems by investing in hybrid computing education and training.

ABOUT THE AUTHOR

 Author and thought leader in the IT field Taylor Royce is well known. He has a two-decade career and is an expert at tech trend analysis and forecasting, which enables a wide audience to understand complicated concepts.

Royce's considerable involvement in the IT industry stemmed from his passion with technology, which he developed during his computer science studies. He has extensive knowledge of the industry because of his experience in both software development and strategic consulting.

Known for his research and lucidity, he has written multiple best-selling books and contributed to esteemed tech periodicals. Translations of Royce's books throughout the world demonstrate his impact.

Royce is a well-known authority on emerging technologies and their effects on society, frequently requested as a speaker at international conferences and as a guest on tech podcasts. He promotes the development of ethical technology, emphasizing problems like data privacy and the digital divide.

In addition, with a focus on sustainable industry growth, Royce mentors upcoming tech experts and supports IT education projects. Taylor Royce is well known for his ability to combine analytical thinking with technical know-how. He sees a time when technology will ethically benefit humanity.

www.ingramcontent.com/pod-product-compliance
Lightning Source LLC
LaVergne TN
LVHW051715050326
832903LV00032B/4223